D1269570

THE Lioness AWAKENS

Lauren Eden

Castle Point Books
New York

THE LIONESS AWAKENS.

Copyright © 2018 by Lauren Eden.

All rights reserved.
Printed in the United States of America.
For information, address
St. Martin's Press, 175 Fifth Avenue,
New York, N.Y. 10010.

www.stmartins.com
www.castlepointbooks.com

The Castle Point Books trademark is owned
by Castle Point Publishing, LLC.
Castle Point books are published and distributed
by St. Martin's Press.

Cover design by Katie Jennings Campbell
Interior design by Joanna Williams
Edited by Monica Sweeney

ISBN 978-1-250-20872-9 (trade paperback)
ISBN 978-1-250-20873-6 (ebook)

Our books may be purchased in bulk for
promotional, educational, or business use.
Please contact your local bookseller or the
Macmillan Corporate and Premium Sales Department
at 1-800-221-7945, extension 5442, or by email
at MacmillanSpecialMarkets@macmillan.com.

First Edition: November 2018

10 9 8 7 6 5 4 3 2 1

DEDICATION

To the rogue lions
that chose the wild

and for River (Vita),
my lioness,

for leading me back
to the pride.

"I know hope—
it is in spite of all
I know of men or death or me."

Erica Jong
At the Edge of the Body

I AM A LIONESS running out of lives. I need the fingers from both hands now to count how many times I've died, and almost all have been at the teeth of lions. But not one hurt more than not being protected by one of my own.

A lioness forced to fight lions as a cub survives only by becoming a lion herself—becoming to herself the father she wished she'd had to protect her. But slowly, as time

1

passes and healing begins, her

survival-mane starts to fall out

one strand of hair at a time as she

learns to shed her aggression, her

fight, her masculinity, her *lion,* to

live again as the lioness she was

born to be. Learning that her

softness is not weakness. Learning

to make love again, not war, and

knowing the difference.

PREY

LIABILITY

I'm afraid I have attracted
more moths than flowers with
    this light.

PARANOID

They tell me
I'm being paranoid
but I am convinced
a woman gave me life
and men
have been trying
to kill me
ever since.

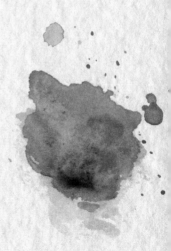

DEBT

They tell me
I am *beautiful*
then stand there
waiting
as though
it owes them
something.

SPORT

When you look like a kill,
all Bambi legs
and deer-in-the-headlights
   stare,
you look like you're game
whether you are
ready
or not.

HEADS OR TAILS

I am like a coin
they flip
from my back
to my stomach.
On one side
I am love,
the other
I am war.

PRESENT

It was like
looking at the sea
and being told
it was green
the way they
wrapped up hate
in pretty paper
and called it
love.

ARMOR

I look in the mirror
armed with my soldiers
of lipstick and mascara
with only one mission
in mind:
How to look less dead.

TEENAGE HEROES

I think back sometimes
to those boys at school
I let them put their hands up
  my skirt
for a cheap thrill
while I chewed gum
and looked the other way
like it was no big deal
because I was dying at home
and truth be told
all those boys at school
with a spare fifteen minutes
to hold me, saved me.

QUICK FIXES

I pop men
like pills
to make me happy,
but they all
wear off
in the end.

LESS

You didn't owe me
anything more
because I took off
my clothes for you,
but I need you to know
that you didn't owe me
any less either.

WITCH HUNT

Those same fingers that
    stroked me tenderly in the
    night, from my neck down to
    the small of my back, are
    pulling me apart this
    morning. In a frantic witch
    hunt through the dark
    forest of my bones; firing
    arrows into the soft, fleshy
    meat of my heart, where he
    wants to cut out all the men
    that came before him; his
    palm, open and waiting, is
    demanding I spit out their
    names like apple seeds.

Who were they? How many?

His hands wave at my chest,
    searching for the guest
    book.

Who came before you? I repeat,
    taking one step forward,
    unflinching, my eyes cold
    and hard like bullets and
    shoot him down. *Love did.*

DIFFERENT

You shift in your seat
to get comfortable.
I shift in my skin.
Please don't tell me we are
    the same.

D.O.A

Men hurt me before I had the
chance to love one.

BROKEN HOME

I spent hours
on my knees
as a child
making dollhouses
out of cardboard boxes
gluing together
scraps of cloth
to make blankets
to keep them warm
and not once
did I make one
of my dolls cry
or make one scared
to fall asleep
in her own bed—

don't tell me I was
too young to know
any different.
I was born with
the meaning of home
running through
my veins.

DECONSTRUCT

You are not
a child anymore.
You should know better
than to pull
a woman apart
just to see how she works.

INVADED

I was peace
and you brought war.
I'd never had a man
call it love before.

COLLATERAL DAMAGE

Sometimes we are just the
  collateral damage
in someone else's war against
  themselves.

ROAM

We are the ones who found
more peace in the wild—
fugitive lionesses
roaming without prides
tough and beaten
not scared of the streets
not when we felt
that much fear at home.

CRIMINALS

I couldn't tell you the names
of everyone I've loved—
they are a blur of giddiness—
but I could pick out
the face of every single
person who's hurt me
in a lineup.

EDITS

It wasn't until I could
read my own fairytales
that I knew my mother
had been lying.
I know she'd edited out
that big bad wolf.

MASOCHISM

Loving you became just
a different way to hate
  myself.

CLARITY

You told me
you would protect me
always
not understanding
that mostly
it would mean
protecting me
from you.

SWALLOW

I've been bitten too
  many times
by the men with golden
  tongues
hissing pretty words in
  my ear
like snakes
urging me to take a bite
but I have lost my appetite
for Adam's apple—
a throat
bulging with tiny
black seeds of cyanide
like lies
not even he
can swallow.

ADRIFT

I lost myself in men
like they were the ocean
and I was adrift.
That is what happens
when a siren loses
her voice.

PRIZE

To live life through the flesh
is to submit to the hunter.

MAGICIAN

For my final trick
I show you my skin
and watch you
dis a p p ea r
by morning.

DARK CIRCLES

I like to keep my darkness
  close
circling
right under
my eyes
stalking my face
just out of
sight.

YOUNG

They're all looking for
someone to grow old with
and I am looking for the one
who can make me feel
like a child again.

DAMAGED

A man almost destroyed me
so I chose the next one
so hellbent on destroying
  himself
he wouldn't have the strength
to hurt me.
It was then I learned
of collateral damage.

PUNCH-DRUNK

Love was you
sitting in the armchair
a bottle in one hand
cigarette in the other
and I on your lap
wishing you
would hold me.

BRUISES

He lives rough. His days are not so gentle on me, like splintered wood rubbing against silk. It hurts. It hurts to see the way he drinks like a fish and still drowns. Hands shaking in his lap. Words like gentle homicides. But when he loves, he is delicate. You should see the flowers unfold like paper. They are as in love with him as I am—their love is written all over their petals, and mine on my face.

He kisses like the wind. His hands, like birds in my hair. He moves inside me like a prayer; rolling over afterwards like he's lost faith the moment I get up to open the window. He thinks

I'm going to fly away again,
but I'm just trying to
breathe. *He's hard to
breathe in.* He tastes like
cigarettes and death—a slow
suicide I can't look away
from.

And I leave with bruises.
Purple orbs from my arms
too tight across my chest
trying not to revolve my
whole world around him; my
flight pattern marked upon
my arms like track marks.

*This is no joy ride, my
kamikaze pilot, my bomb;
always going off to war
with you.*

37

SAFE

He'd always ask me
if I felt safe with him
so many times
I began to question
why he so badly
needed to hear it.

TRAMPLED

O maiden moon
how the men walked all
  over you
just to prove
that they could.

REVENGE

I prey on married men
who remind me of my father
with wives
who look like
the woman
who took him away
from me
splitting them apart
in carefully considered ways—
ways I was never considered.

WHITE KNIGHTS

My biggest fright was
   finding out
that even the men who were good
were not always good.
I'd been looking for the men
with sharp teeth and
   narrowed eyes
looking at me like a meal.
I didn't know that it was
   the men
with hands gentler than my own
with voice boxes filled
   with honey
men who sharpened
their knives on diamonds
and fed me little white lies
that tasted like sugar going
   down—
that these would be the men
who would hurt me most.

TANGLED

I wonder of other women. How
they might untangle their
bodies softly from their
lovers' after they make
love, delicately, like
unknotting two necklaces
twisted together in a
jewelry box. Women who let
a man linger a little longer
inside them, like a hand
pausing mid-air in
farewell.

I wonder of women like me.
Women who rip their bodies
away quickly afterward,
like a band-aid covering a
wound he thought he could
kiss all better (the wound
that never gets better).

Women who snatch
themselves away angrily
like a child who doesn't
want to share herself
anymore. Women who roll out
of a man's arms as
naturally as other women
roll in; their eyes fixed
dreamily on his chest while
ours stare idly at the wall,
fixed, as the rest of us lies
broken.

WANT

Some days it hurts
and I need to remember this
on the days that it doesn't.
Remember
to protect my thin skin
on the days I wear mine
thick like armor.
Remember
that on the nights
he feels like a vacation
he will feel like an abandoned
  house
in the morning.
Remember
that on the days
I am stuck in his honey

I will wake in the morning
eyes stinging
from wanting him.
Remember
that he only wants me
some of the time
when I've only
ever wanted him
always.

MUTUAL

I kissed a man's neck last
　night
for the first time in as
　long as
I can remember
and I thought
finally
after all this time
I am beginning
to see sex
as something I do
and not something
that is done to me.

TOGETHER

He came to me
with his hands deep
inside his pockets
ashamed
of the dirt hidden
behind his fingernails
and I held them in mine
palm
to palm
and with the warmth
we made
he grew flowers.

FIX

There's a theory that says
if you don't fix a broken
  window
within a couple of days
you will invite vandals
and if people work
in the same way
then I've only got
one more day
to get over you.

CAPTIVITY

STARVED

When you are not fed love on
   a silver spoon
you learn to lick it off
   knives.

FIRST

I feel his mouth
closing in.
I lick my lips quickly
to get to me first.

TOO CLOSE

It was your breath
warm and beating
on the back of my neck
erupting my skin
in a shiver
that I now recognize
as a reaction of fear—
you
standing too close
for me to breathe.

OPEN

I envy birds
how their home
has no ceiling
how they never
outgrow their lives
never bump their heads
never stoop
never crouch
never fold up smaller
to fit through doors
the world insists
they walk through.

TINY

I cannot fathom
how I could ever
have shrunk
so small to live
in the palm of
a hand.

CHASE

I'm afraid that he could have
the warmest hands
and I would still
slip between his fingers.
The truth is I've been slipping
since the day a man
put his hands on me—
when I was too young
and hadn't yet found the joy
in keeping still
and now love feels
like just a *wriggle-away*
like a game of hide and seek
like the cat and mouse pursuit
of a girl who likes to
  be chased
much more than she likes
to be caught.

COLD

It was like standing
in front of the moon
like you would the sun
and expecting it to
warm you.

SPRAY PAINT

It is not love
to graffiti yourself on men
who are like brick walls,
to throw yourself
like paint at their cold
hard chests trying
to make art,
to fingerprint
on the walls
of a house
that will never
feel like home.
That is not love.
That is vandalism.

TEARS

I think I'm crying
for all the men
who can't—
it seems the only way I can
  explain it
how they can look at me
with eyes as hollow and dry
as empty cups
while I *pour*
neither glasses
half full
nor empty.

MIGRATE

Like a migrating bird leaves
when there is no fruit left
on the tree
I'll go where it's warm.
I won't stay
to die with you.

CONDIMENTS

His rummaging through me
is not gentle.
No matter how carefully
he turns things over—
it is an invasion
I say
to force your way through
    doors
I keep closed behind me
wanting more
always more
looking for salt
when I've put
the sugar bowl
in front of you.

HALF-CAF

He would order me
at half-strength if he could.
Like a weaker coffee
a customer custom-orders
from the barista
who shares an eye-roll
with the man next in line
who I wish were next in line
for me.

STAINED

I can smell fear as well as
the next dog. I smelled it on
him like cheap cologne and
napalm. I told myself all
men smelled that way. I'd
smelled it on my father the
week before he left my
mother, leaving behind an
air of entitlement and
unpaid telephone bills.

It is the scent of the free
man. Wild grass, trickling
sweat and tobacco. It is the
scent of motor oil and gas
when he slams his foot on
the accelerator, leaving
puffs of smoke like empty
speech bubbles. It is the
scent of sex with girls who
look nothing like you,
lipstick-stained wine
glasses and fresh lingerie

off the line—a scent so
heavy you can't blow it out
of your nose for weeks. It
permeates. It stains. It
reeks, and I smelled it,
stronger, whenever I'd lean
in closer asking him never
to leave me. And I smelled it
strongest, that day in June
when I asked him if one day
he thought he might ever
want to marry me. I followed
it, its trail, circling the
front of his door as he left
me on my knees, begging
him, *I can give you more
time. I can wait a little
longer.*

And here I am, still on them,
scrubbing out the smell of
broken dreams from his
carpet.

SHARE

A pretty cover
makes them hover
like a man reading
another man's newspaper
over his shoulder.
And a man doesn't like
to share his newspaper
any more than he likes
to share his woman
so he closes her,
narrows her
just wide enough
for his eyes only
until the men beside him
lose interest
and vow to find another.

FREE

It is the way
I pull away from him
when he kisses me
my hair wound gently in
  his fist
that tells me
I will always fight for
  freedom
in even the most
beautiful capture.

TRUST

Watch how the sky keeps
   the stars
in his sight without
   holding them.

CAPRICIOUS

I want you all to myself,
he says.
They all say it soon enough
but I've never
been a loyal girl—
I love in moon
and not in star
coming to them
a little less
a little more
each night.

GOOD GIRL

You can sieve the stars from
the sky
and glue them together to
make a moon
and it may fool you
for awhile—
Is a light not just a light?
But you will start to see the
cracks
like the veins you traced
inside his arms
from the right one you let go

because your mother
and your father
and your god told you so
and now your heart
is a dark place
it is a hopeless abyss
where your heart sinks
cleanly like a stone
making no ripples
like the good girl
you are.

STICKY SITUATIONS

Beautiful women are like bees
stuck in their very own honey.

STRANGE

Is it strange to have
men look at you all day?
he asked.
No. But it would be strange
  of me
to notice.

NAKED

I outgrew romantic love long
   ago. Like a favorite sweater
   I kept putting back on
   because I remembered once
   when it kept me warm. When
   I once felt good in it.
   Before it became riddled
   with holes like a badly told
   lie. Before it felt heavy on
   my shoulders, like the world
   was putting pressure on me
   to get it right.

I had to say, *enough, enough.* I
   can't breathe. I can't move.
   I can't pretend any longer
   that this is what I want.

I want to be bare. Bold.
Truth-telling. Absolute,
without the filling in of
another. I want to be like
the wind, naked and free,
running through the gaps of
fingers, blowing up skirts,
ruffling the ends of hair,
without ever getting caught.

THE PRINCESS AND THE PEA

I crave the fire
the one that blazes in a
  man's eyes
when I take off my dress
and let him do the rest.
I crave deadly reds
and tangerine dreams
hungry hands down
the front of my jeans
and I don't know what
transpires in my mind—

this desire of the weakest
    kind
to be needed from the
    outside in
my heart—a pea
beneath these distracting
layers of flesh
that men lie upon in the night
as I lie awake
hoping by morning
they'll feel it.

Q&A

We curve
like a question mark
to fit the shape
of a lover's body
that when alone,
lie simple
and straight
like an answer.

NOTICE

It is easy to call a woman
waving her hands around
hysterical
when a man loves with
his hands over his ears.
That is the language of
    a woman
gone unheard too long.

FLIPSIDE

I had two sides to me
but I could only
see one.
That is what happens
when you only hear
your mother's side
of your story.

PARADOX

He is the only one I could give
up my power to
because he is the only one who
has never asked.

CIRCLES

Men broke me. And now I love
broken men. A sick, full
circle that makes me dizzy
and gets me nowhere. Men
who have moments of loving
me so purely they surprise
themselves like a hiccup.
It's that surprise. I'm
addicted to that surprise.
As though they never knew
they had it in them, and
here I am pulling love out
of their mouths like ribbon.
I am a magician. *Look at
what's inside you. Look at
all this magic.*

I want to call their mothers.
Their fathers. Tell them,
*Look at what your boy is
capable of. Look what you
could've grown in him had
you watered him every day
with the same devotion with*

*which you poured liquor
down your throats. (No, you
never forgot to do that.)*
And here he is. This man.
Rising each morning for me
like a sun. Tucking my hair
behind my ear. Writing me
poetry.
But when it falls apart, it
falls apart good. Like a
hurricane of misery
sweeping through me—my
life in ruins. This man
knows how to hurt, and when
I hurt him, I look like every
goddamned person who let
him down, unrecognizable
in his lineup, like a mural
of pain with faces all
blurred into one. And that
is when the darkness comes.
Deeper and darker—a
fiercer devil than I'd ever

encountered in those angel
boys I loved.

But it's always worth it,
somehow. My hand on the
side of his face reminding
him, *It's me. It's me. It's not
them, it's me. Come back to
me.* And there it is. Those
two lights turn on in his
eyes like flashlights in a
derelict house. And it's time
for me to plant flowers
again.

LIGHT

The less you require of love
the lighter love gets.
I once told a man
he didn't need to build a life
  with me.
I didn't need him to be
  husband material;
pay my mortgage
mow my lawn—
he just needed to be *the love
  of my life*
and you should've seen
his whole body sigh
rising like smoke
from dead wood in the fire.

LOST

I lose one
I lose them all
these domino men
falling all over again
flat on their backs
like bugs the wrong
side up
like a coin
that never brings
me luck—*fuck*
I lose one
I lose them all.

HOVER

I will not let a man
hover over me
like a coat he insists
I cover up with.
I've always thought
I was best dressed
with bedroom eyes
with a strut
that could outrun
freedom.

COMMIT

Some moths
fly to lanterns
while some fly
straight to the fire.
But is it really a life
if we are not killed
by the very thing
we desire?

SHARED

You are not meant
to be kept close
to a man's chest
like a secret.
You are meant
to be shared
until the world
is whispering of you.

ADVICE

The wind
caresses my arms
like a familiar lover.
My skin aquiver
at her confessions
as she whispers in my ear
everything I need to know
about letting go.

SHARPENING
THE CLAWS

TASTE

I am not bitter
nor am I sweet—
I am water
and how
I taste to you
depends on what
you mix me with.

NATURAL

I'm tired of getting pretty
   for you.
The ocean
doesn't color
herself blue.

REFLECTIONS

Men are lousy mirrors.
Rather than reflecting
my innermost workings
my fears
my daddy issues
I stop instead
to fix my hair.

FED

Men think I'm not interested
because I'm not dying
  of hunger
for them
but they've got me wrong
I *am* hungry
I just keep myself
well-fed these days.

IMAGINATION

They never feel quite real
and that's because they're not.
I dream them
I create them.
They are out of this world!
My head—
an overgrown terrarium
where fantasy men
grow wild and fast
like bamboo.

FAIRYTALES

I was always suspicious
of those *Happily Ever Afters*.
The way they disappeared
off the page without a trace
with no other pages
as evidence.

LEAVE

I've been saying goodbye
to the men in my family
since I learned how to wave.
You will have to threaten me
with a little more than that
to shake me.

AFRAID

You think you are
fighting with me
but you are fighting
with yourself
because I am love
and you need to figure out
why you keep walking
out on it.

DOMINANCE

They don't want us to take
  a stand
when they think we belong on
  our knees.

MARKED

I couldn't hide
the bite marks
the scratches up my thighs
the kind of
territorial evidence
men want other men
to notice.

NO

From the moment
you balled your tiny fists
at their chests
they said you'd be a handful
and from the day
you learned to say, *No,*
they knew you'd be more
than a mouthful, too.
But you are a hurricane,
you are a flood
you are the reminder
that being too much
for the world
still has its place.

SUBSTITUTE

When you find yourself
    intimidated
by a woman's strength,
ask her how many men
she had to become
to stand in for the ones
who left.

EGGSHELLS

I don't want
to be your dream girl
walking on eggshells
trying not to slip
on the yolk of who I am
careful not to wake you.

BUSINESS

If he tells you
you tick all his boxes
as though women are
  checklists
designed to meet a man's
  expectations
he will not love you like
  poetry—
that man means
strictly business.
Tell him he has no business
being with you.

HEARD

I made listening to myself
a priority
over needing
to be heard
when I learned
that no matter
how eloquently
my dreams spoke
sex always spoke
over the top of me.

SNARE

I leave knots in my hair
as a snare
for the men who run
their fingers through it
expecting me to be
silken and behaved.
One *good girl*
and their hand
is mine
like a Venus flytrap
that's captured Mars.

WRITTEN

You would've liked me better
    five years ago. I didn't like
    myself much. I was an
    outline, colored in by boys
    who couldn't keep between
    the lines—a piece of paper
    with a rough sketch, drawn
    by an unsteady hand that
    knew nothing about art,
    even less of the power I had
    inside me to be an artist. I
    only knew survival. I only
    knew how to fold up small.

And so I folded. I became a
    paper plane, when I
    should've been a swan, one
    that would fly right out of
    here, only to return at
    moonlight crumpled into a
    ball, small enough to sleep
    inside a man's palm, if one
    was open for me—his legs
    crossed over mine like

scissors; rocks in my head.
Always choosing men who
wanted to make something
out of me. Because there was
no writing on my wall yet,
only loud graffiti painted
by territorial men wanting
to claim me.

You would've liked me better
five years ago. You would've
been exactly my type. But
now I am **written**. Clearly. In
bold. I *cry* in italics. <u>I am
love</u>, underlined. My words
lean in so closely to hear
what I've got to say next,
there is not enough space
to slip yours between them.
The years have unfolded me.
I have been told.

INTOLERANCE

Boy,
you can certainly
hold your liquor
but love
that is one intoxicant
you don't seem to have
the stomach for.

SPOTLIGHT

It doesn't excite me
to be desired
in a sneaky sideways
glance.
Not when I know
how it feels
to have a man
unable to take
his eyes off of me.

PUDDLES

He tells me
my eyes look
like oceans
and I tell him
they are just puddles
that too many dirty feet
have splashed in.

REBELLIOUS

He says
I'm easy on the eyes
but hard to swallow.
Simple lips
but tough talk
like meat stuck in molars
and maybe
that will keep
the sheep at bay
while the wolves can play
howling at the moon
in honor of her
rebellious cycles—
him, still flirting
with the stars
and all of her
pretty likenesses.

DIGNITY

I can try to convince you of
   many things
but loving me will not be one
   of them.

PORTRAIT OF A LADY

You thought I would always
  be there
hanging
like a portrait
on your wall
wearing
a cracked smile
with eyes
that never leave you
but I was never
the kind of girl
to sit idly on a couch
waiting for a man to be done
despite your insistence
for me to be painted
in that way.

CLOTH

Wife material. I've heard this
    term since I reached
    puberty. Since boys started
    taking an interest in me
    and my mother noticed.

And I've always wondered—
    what kind of texture is wife
    material? Is it papery like
    the ancient texts that
    celebrate it? Is it crispy
    like the carrots and
    broccoli she prepares for
    Sunday roast? Silky like the
    negligees she wears in bed
    to seduce her husband?

I've always known that I
    wasn't cut from the same
    cloth. Mine is made from
    the thorn of dandelion.

Crusty and tough like the misbehaving moon. Coarse and sinewy like meat that gets stuck between your teeth. I am not a soft landing. I will leave a scar. But you will have a story to tell around the campfire.

DIFFICULT

They tell me I'm difficult
as though I am only
making it harder
for myself.
But I'm not.
Being difficult
has always
come easily to me.

MOTHER

A strange thing happens
when a woman tells a man off
for his bad behavior.
He shuts up. He apologizes.
She becomes his mother.

COMPLICATED

You're only complicated to
   a man
who simply wants to fuck you.

DREAMCATCHER

They tell me
to live my dreams
as though it is simple
to a woman
who wakes each morning
tangled and half-strangled
in her dreamcatcher.
I'm just trying not to be my
worst nightmare.

CHOSEN

I'm not impressed
when a man tells me he
    wants me
when he asks me out on a date
when he tells me
I'm pretty—
the sun shines on me
every damn day I wake
each moment I hear life
breathing in and out of me
I know that I was chosen.

JACQUELINE IN A BOX

With my passions quelled
I fell into my mold
like a Girl Scout cookie
to be sold to the mothers
   of sons
with eyes like the devil.
Crumbling to the world
and its demands to behave
like some pretty,
ready-made doll thing
out of a box
winding me up in ways
that told them I was beyond
saving
but no one puts
Jacqueline in a box
without getting a little scared.

SPICE

I take men with a pinch
   of salt these days;
it is women who have
   the sugar.

VALIDATED

The moment you were born,
your presence was validated.
You don't need a second
  opinion.

ASS-ONISTS

I am not responsible
for putting out the fires
kindled by men who can't
control their matchsticks.

DEVOUR

I don't take small bites.
I either devour you
or I push the plate away.

SETTLED

Every time I think
I've settled the score,
I recount the tally
and I am always
just a little behind.
I am always
one man away
from being settled.

NINE LIVES

SHADOW

My mother always warned me
about the tall, dark stranger.
She never told me
she was talking about
my shadow.

GHOST

They tell me I am cold
and I beg them,
please be patient.
I am a haunted house
trying so very hard
to be a home.

LANTERNS

I wake up angry,
each day
cut out for me
into shreds,
and I make lanterns—
paper lanterns
to hang
before the moon
pulls me back
into her shadows,
dawn searching for me
like a flashlight,
and I have to begin
all over again.

TERMINAL

He said,
Tell me how I can help.
I said,
Just make me comfortable.
This pain is terminal.

MISTRESS

Sadness was always
the mistress between us.
I'm sorry I could never get
  her to leave.

BREATHE

That hardness
that coldness
lodged
in the center of me
is a thousand tears
I could not cry
and one day
I will cry every
single one of them
and I will learn
to breathe again.

PERSPECTIVE

Life is short,
they say.
Life is short
like a quick burst of light
and maybe so
for the ones
who have not lived days
as long and dark
as shadows.

NUMB

Nobody ever told me
that feeling nothing
would be the most
exhausting feeling of all.

EVERYTHING

I said,
I've been hurt in ways
your mind doesn't want
to think about,
and your heart—
I'm afraid what I tell you
will blow it out like a candle
and you will find out
   just what
real darkness feels like.
So stand there in the doorway
with that slow, sleepy smile
and tell me again
that you want to know
everything about me.

PARAPHRASES

I am learning to tell
my tragic tales
like comedies
by changing just
a few short words.
Sometimes survival is
  that simple.

NURSE ON CALL

I've come back from the dead
so many times that I don't
   struggle
with the pain.
I put myself to bed.
I gather flowers.
I stroke my own head.

SOFT SPOTS

I am the strongest person
    I know.
I know all
my soft spots
yet still
don't have
the power
to break me.

HEXAGONS

When I flash
this sweet-as-honey
smile at you
please know
the work I've had to put in
to ordering this mess
of my heart
into hexagons.

RUNNING

We run
into arms
to countries
to vices
telling ourselves
we are searching
for ourselves
when really, we're just
    running
running as fast as we can
before our sadness
    catches up.

DEAF

It was the love
they all spoke about
and I had gone deaf.

WORN

Love knocked on my door to
  play today
and I gave her an apology.
I didn't make an excuse.
I didn't say
I had other plans
or that I simply
couldn't.
I told her the truth:
I'm tired.

THE YOUNGEST TIRED PEOPLE

We were the youngest
tired people
you could ever meet
secret lives hidden under our
  fingernails
hurts welded into scars
living through enough pain
to be almost dead
in love with people
who'd barely felt enough
to be alive.

BOULDER

I want you to know—
this heavy thing I am
    carrying—
not to carry it
just
know it.

TIDY

You wouldn't believe the
　things
I've forgiven people for
but don't think I'm kind—
the way I help sweep up
　their mess.
I just prefer to live in a
　tidy home.

CANYON

I had mistaken him
for all the things I aspired to
peace
paradise
oneness
but he was simply love
and I had become so empty
that love was no longer
  enough
to fill me.

NO CASUALTIES

We talk about love
not ruining us anymore
and our mouths are sad
our voices whisper
when we say it.
Love does not ruin me anymore
because indeed
it was rather romantic
to think about—
love being the death of us.
But she is merely an injury
and we will succumb
to illness and age
like the rest of them.

WATER

I don't seek the fire anymore
but I'll still
sit by it some nights
under moonlight
with a boy whose eyes
glow amber like a wolf's.
But it is water now
that calls me
the frothing river mouth
the bitter sea
the quiet bay of my soul
I bathe in.

ORIGIN

Let the heat of your tears
   remind you
that they've come from a
   warm place.

KINDNESS

Just as a bee dies
after it stings
so does a part of us
each time we choose
hurt over honey.

ENDINGS

Forevers are for princesses
and endings
for goddesses.
They know it's where
they begin.

APOCALYPSE

Tell me
as the world is ending
that there is someone
worth saving before yourself
and I will tell you,
you're a fool.
You could've saved
the whole damn world
when it was alive
if you had only loved
yourself that much.

EVOLUTION

Anything that doesn't evolve—
people
love
dreams—
anything
that tries to keep still
while the earth revolves
gets flattened
next time
it comes around.

THE KINDEST THING

I wouldn't say
I am overtly kind
but inwardly
I am doing
the kindest thing
I can do for this world,
and that is heal.
We don't need any more broken
  bodies.

CONFESSIONS

I confess
I loved you more
than I let on
but you weren't
ready for it
and I wasn't going
to pour myself
into hands
that couldn't
hold me.

SURRENDER

Let go.
Fruit that clings
to the tree
rots.
You taste sweetest when
  you fall.

BELIEF

I've lost count
of how many times
I've looked in the mirror
and told myself
it was all going to be okay.
But I can only count
on one hand
how many times
I have believed it.

ALONE

Sometimes the best thing
that can ever happen to us
is to feel alone in this world
because when you make it
through to the other side
you will love yourself for it
in ways
you only ever gave
to someone else.

THE MIDDLE

I'd only ever left love when it
ended. But with you, I left
in the middle. Still in love
with you. So ever in love
with you. Packing up my
things while my heart clung
to your chest, wailing like
a child.

And I don't know what kind of
strength the world blessed
me with in that moment. I'm
convinced it would've been
easier to tear a bird from
the sky with my bare hands.
Maybe it was angels. Maybe
it was simply my survival
instinct kicking in,

knowing that I couldn't stay to die with you. I was not made to stay in that kind of darkness. If I were, I would've died before my twelfth birthday. All I knew was that I was too old and too strong to let a man take me down now.

PEACE

Once I felt peace
surging through
my fingertips, I knew
there would never
be a pair of hands
that could tempt me
back into chaos.

PORTAL

Sometimes
when I squint
really hard
I can see myself
in every one
I try to love.

SURVIVAL

I shot myself
in the heart
with Cupid's arrow
and they called it
a suicide attempt.
They don't know
a life survival skill
when they see one.

HOPE

That sliver of light
beneath the door—
that one strip of hope
my eyes cling to
in the darkness.
I find it. I always do.

SIMPLE

Life is simple.
Say it.
Then listen
to all those voices,
not your own
interrupting,
trying to complicate it
for you.

YIN AND YANG

I counted on one hand
those who had loved me most
then counted on the other
those who had hurt me the
  deepest
and when I clasped them
both together
I could see that peace
had come to me at last.

SOFTNESS

Succumb to me.
Leave your battles
with the boys and
let me wrap you up
in the white flag
of my sheets
surrendering you
to a softness
we don't have to
tell anyone about—
your rough hands
never looked
so gentle
under candlelight.

FRICTION

I've lost too much.
I don't have anything left
  to burn.
Everything I have now
I fought the wildfires for
and I recognize that friction
in our skin when it touches
that blaze in your eyes
stirring up my ashes.
You are the kind of risk
I just won't take anymore.

AWAKENING

Waking
can feel like
an inconvenience
when you'd planned
on sleepwalking
through the rest
of your life.

RETURNING

I am returning
slowly
to the hollow
of my oak
finding my way back
through the dark forest
  of men
their torsos carved with
  my initials
men
who offered me shelter
from all the storms
that weren't my own.
But it is time, now.
It is time to come home.

RITUAL

Women might
ebb and flow
like moon tides
but we want a man
to love us like the sun
arriving on time
and always,
always
with breakfast.

STRIP

You ask me why
I like to undress myself
in front of you
and I tell you
it is my only power play
in a world
that is always trying
to undress me
first.

PARADISE

The easy lives
get harder
while the hard lives
get easier
and I can tell you
this ninth life
is a dream.

PRIDE

MINE

I was given
the most valuable
brutal lesson
of them all
and it was this:
I had to leave
the love of my life
to save myself.
I left the love of my life
for me.
And in making
that choice
I became
the love of my life.

HIGHER PURPOSE

I caught the one I was
    made for
red-handed in the garden
dirt on his hands
trying to bury my rib
back into the earth
muttering to God,
She is not what I wanted—
and that was when I knew
that perhaps I was made
for something different
in this life.
Maybe something more.

CONSENT

Our bodies heal without
   permission,
but our hearts need consent.
   Give it.

WORTHY

I am worthy of light
of warmth.
The sun tells me so
each morning
no matter
how many times the moon
shrugs her cold shoulders
at me.

BIOLOGY

As a woman
I am always aware
my womb is empty
that I am not filled
but I am starting to know
the difference now
between the pang
of my biology
and the true aching
of loneliness.

OCCUPIED

Claim yourself.
Plant flowers
upon the sill
of your lashes
hang signs
from your mouth
like a door.
Let them know
you are cared for.
Let them know
someone is home.

TOTALITY

There was never another love
I needed more than my own.

PROGRESS

The past is meant to be
  re-visited
preferably
with a friend
and a glass of wine
opening secrets
like candy wrappers
letting their bittersweet
  tastes
settle on your tongue
before spitting them
back out again
and that is where you
  leave it—
you kiss it goodbye.
You never
see it again.

GRACE

I love how butterflies just
    flap their wings
without needing to talk
    about it.

MERCY

I am mostly easy to love
but when
I am not
don't make it
harder on me.

IMMORTAL

It is the crackle you hear
from the fire burning you
down to the ground
that is your spirit;
cracking like a whip
under your skin
still alive
still blazing—
the sound
of your magic.

GOLD

Sometimes
we hand ourselves over
to someone we love
on a silver platter
and they still don't want us
and maybe
that is the problem.
We forget we are gold.

LESSONS

I will tell my daughter:

You will be worshipped. The wrong men will fall at your feet. You will be demeaned, envied—by strangers, best friends, sisters, your mother. You will not be seen—your intelligence, your kindness—overlooked. You will be bullied, may become prey to the fathers of friends, brothers of friends (you will think it is your fault).

You may not ever have a platonic friendship with a man, but you will be loved many times over by men. Many of whom won't care to really know you.

But what will make you feel
most alone is being told by
the world that these
problems make you lucky. It
doesn't. But you mustn't
downplay your beauty. You
should have fun with it.
Celebrate it. You don't need
to make excuses for it, but
you do need to be aware of
the effect it has on the
people around you, because
once you are aware of its
effect, you will never take
any reactions to it to
heart. You will set it free.
Only then will you see how
very little it means at all.

COLD

I've been told my entire life,
I'm *cold*
because I've never
needed anyone to warm me.
How do they not see the
paradox in that?
Now they tell me it is
this kind of aloofness
this indifference
this nonchalance
that makes me *cool*.
I've been a fire this
whole time.

REVIVAL

These men
feel like the death of me
and it is always women
over coffee and
over wine
bringing me back
to life again.

HONEST

I look at the moon
and I don't ask her
how her night's been.
I know
just by looking at her
that she is not
holding her breath
any more than I am.

IMPOSSIBLE

*You give your love away
   too easily,*
that is what
they tell you
and only you know why
because it has always
felt impossible
to give it to yourself.

REVOLUTION

Women are punished
for celebrating their
  sexuality
when they should be
celebrating with us
that despite the efforts
to get us to hate
our bodies,
we love them—
we enjoy them.

KINGDOM

You think I look
like a queen from the outside?
Well I can assure you
that on
the inside
I am the whole
fucking kingdom.

WILD

I tie myself
into knots over you
thinking of how
your fingers are going
to unravel me,
my clever
big-boy scout.
This is what you'd been
preparing yourself for.
It was never about
learning to survive in the
  wild.
It was about losing yourself
  in it.

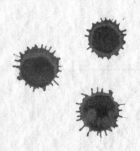

RAW

You did to me
what I thought
could never be done.
You loved me
and I felt
every
single
bit of it.

SEXUAL HEALING

I smile when we make love now.
I am forgetting the
memories. Washed clean the
touch of my hunters from my
skin. Wiped away the faces I
used to pull like the girls
in those videos. Like I am
in pain. Like I am scared.
Like I really don't want it.
Covered my ears from all
those *Beg for me*s and *I
want to make you scream*s.
It tastes like honey. It
feels like sunlight.

SUNSET

I am the light
in your eyes
and I will be
taking it with me
when I leave.

FRIENDSHIP

We talk of men
like we talk of sport,
licking each other's paws,
lazy stories
falling from our yawns,
and we love them
we really do love them—
but in the way we watch
the hot sun slipping below
the horizon
with relief,
finding as much joy
in their goodbye
as we did in their hello.

READY

A lot can happen in 28 days.
Just ask the moon. In one,
ask the sun.

They say it takes 21 days to
break a habit. But how many
years does it take to
unlearn everything that's
been taught to you since
you were a child? Love
taught to us by people who
hated themselves.

How many generations will it
take for a man to soak the
war off his skin? How many
more generations will
women have to keep running
the bath—coaxing a man to
bathe in warmth and
softness, letting his wounds
soak in lavender and honey?

They say life moves in seven-
year cycles, and if I marked
mine on a chart, I would lie

on my stomach like a child with crayons scattered around me in colors I've never seen before, and I would paint this fifth one yellow. Yellow. The color of sun melting in the sky like butter. Yellow. The color of my daughter's pajamas as her small foot slides idly next to mine. Yellow. The color of the long grass a lioness crouches low in, waiting to pounce. That is me. A lioness. Stalking my life before it runs away from me again. I am ready now. Ready to roar. Ready to pounce.